Welcome to the
Disney Learning Programme!

Sharing a book with your children is the perfect opportunity to cuddle and enjoy the reading experience together. Research has shown that reading aloud to and with your children is one of the most important ways to prepare them for success as a reader. When you share books with each other, you help strengthen your children's reading and vocabulary skills as well as stimulate their curiosity, imagination and enthusiasm for reading.

Anyone can be anything in Zootropolis! In this book, Judy fulfils her childhood dream and becomes a police officer. Judy really wants to solve crimes, but she has to start at the bottom and work her way up. She meets Nick, a clever but mischievous fox. Little does she know it, but Nick will be vital to her crime-solving success.

You can help your children enjoy the story even more by talking to them about their hopes and dreams for the future. Ask them about what they might like to do when they grow up. Talk about other books where unlikely characters work together. Remind them of how characters in books are not always what they seem at first. Children who can make connections to other books they have read are able to imagine new stories more fully and enjoy the story more.

Children learn in different ways and at different speeds, but they all require a supportive environment to nurture a lifelong love of books, reading and learning. The Adventures in Reading books are carefully levelled to present new challenges to developing readers. They are filled with familiar and fun characters from the wonderful world of Disney to make the learning experience comfortable, positive and enjoyable.

Enjoy your reading adventure together!

Scholastic Children's Books
Euston House,
24 Eversholt Street,
London NW1 1DB, UK

A division of Scholastic Ltd
London • New York • Toronto • Sydney • Auckland
Mexico City • New Delhi • Hong Kong

This book was first published in the United States in 2016
by Random House Children's Books, a division of Penguin Random House LLC.
This edition published in the UK by Scholastic Ltd, 2016.

ISBN 978 14071 6606 3

Printed in Malaysia

2 4 6 8 10 9 7 5 3 1

Papers used by Scholastic Children's Books are made from woods grown in sustainable forests.

www.scholastic.co.uk

ZOOTROPOLIS

LEVEL 2

DISNEY LEARNING

THE BIG CASE

ADVENTURES IN READING

By Bill Scollon
Illustrated by
the Disney Storybook Art Team

Judy Hopps is a bunny. Her parents want her to be a carrot farmer. Judy dreams of being a police officer.

Judy works hard to make her dream
come true. She is the first bunny to join
the police force.
In Zootropolis anyone can be anything!

Judy says goodbye to her family in Bunnyburrow. She moves to the big city. The city is exciting, noisy and crowded. But everyone gets along!

Judy is happy and proud. She will
be a police officer and help to keep
Zootropolis safe.

Judy reports for duty. She really wants to solve crimes, but her job is to give out parking tickets. She will be the best traffic officer ever!

Judy uses her super-hearing to hear
when the parking meter runs out.
When she is out working, she notices
a fox. She decides to follow him.

Judy finds the fox trying to buy a
Jumbo-pop. The fox is called Nick.
Nick tricks Judy into buying the
Jumbo-pop for his son, Finnick.

Nick melts the Jumbo-pop. He uses it to make little ice-pops, which he sells to lemmings. Finnick is Nick's friend, not his son. Judy has been tricked again!

Back at headquarters, Mr Otterton
is reported missing. Assistant Mayor
Bellwether tells Chief Bogo to give
Judy the case. Judy has her first crime
to solve.

Judy is given a picture. The picture
shows Mr Otterton with one of Nick's
ice-pops. Judy tricks Nick into helping
her with the case.

Nick saw Mr Otterton go into a spa.
Nick and Judy go there. They meet
a yak who says that Mr Otterton left in
a car. The yak remembers the car's
number plate.

Nick knows someone who can help.
Flash can find out who owns the car.
Flash is very slow! It takes hours to get
the address.

The address belongs to Manchas
the jaguar. He lives in the Rainforest
District. He is the driver who picked
up Mr Otterton.

Nick and Judy find Manchas.
Suddenly, he changes.
Manchas becomes a savage beast!
Nick and Judy run for their lives!

Manchas disappears. Judy and Nick search videos of the scene. They see wolves take Manchas away in a van. Nick guesses where they went.

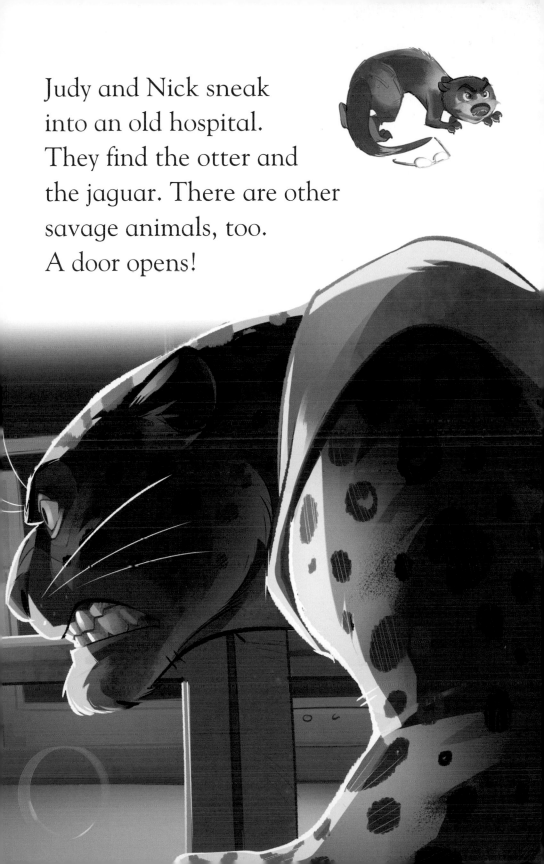

Judy and Nick sneak
into an old hospital.
They find the otter and
the jaguar. There are other
savage animals, too.
A door opens!

It is Mayor Lionheart! He has a
doctor with him. The doctor tells
them that stress turns the animals
into savage beasts.

Mayor Lionheart does not want the city to panic. He has a plan. He will keep the savage animals locked up.

Judy and Nick tell Chief Bogo that
the missing animals are at the hospital.
Mayor Lionheart is arrested for
kidnapping animals.
Bellwether becomes mayor.

The animals in Zootropolis are afraid.
Who will turn savage next?
Nobody gets along – not even Judy
and Nick. Judy quits the police force.

Judy goes back to Bunnyburrow.
Her dad tells her about night howlers.
They are flowers that can make
animals go crazy.

Judy races back to Zootropolis.
She tells Nick that she knows what has
happened. She thinks that someone is
using night howlers to make animals
turn savage.

Judy and Nick find a secret night howler lab. They sneak in and hide. They see that the flowers are being made into a bright blue juice.

Judy and Nick wait. Then they creep through the lab and take some night howler juice.

Nick and Judy hurry to the police station. On the way, Bellwether stops them in the Natural History Museum. She darts Nick with the night howler juice.

Nick is turning savage!
Bellwether wants to make
everyone afraid. Then she
can control the city.

Nick stops. He is not turning savage.
He and Judy switched the night howler
juice for blueberry juice.

It was a trick!
Chief Bogo arrests Bellwether.
Case closed!

Nick joins the police force.
Together, Nick and Judy make a great
team. They will keep Zootropolis safe!